impressions
Charleston

photography and text by Robb Helfrick

FARCOUNTRY
PRESS

In memory of my grandparents, Edward and Madeline Helfrick.

Dedicated to Megan: With love for my sister with the adventurous heart.

COVER: The Morris Island Lighthouse sits perilously close to the shoreline at the entrance to Charleston Harbor.

BACK COVER: Seated in the serene landscape of Middleton Place, the "Wood Nymph" is surrounded by a profusion of summer blossoms.

TITLE PAGE: In a rare daytime sighting, a ghost crab scrambles across the beach at low tide.

RIGHT: Morning brings soft light and warm tones to Waterfront Park on the Cooper River.

BELOW: Sea foam bubbles reflect a variety of colors from the Carolina sky.

ISBN: 1-56037-317-2
Photographs © 2005 by Robb Helfrick
© 2005 Farcountry Press
Text by Robb Helfrick

Created, produced, and designed in the United States.
Printed in China.

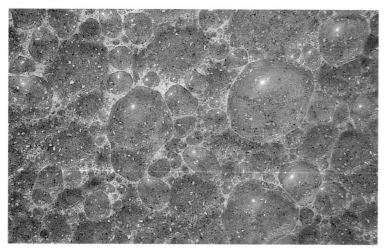

ABOVE: A solitary boat is silhouetted by early sunlight as it sets out for a daybreak cruise on the Atlantic.

FACING PAGE: Delicate yellow blossoms burst forth, mimicking the hue of a stately home in a classic Charleston scene along the East Battery.

Introduction   BY ROBB HELFRICK

My first visit to Charleston happened to fall on the one-hundredth anniversary of the great earthquake of 1886. As a newcomer visiting on that warm and humid August day, I was surprised to learn that a city located on the Atlantic seaboard could suffer such a California-type calamity. The thought of that catastrophic centennial stayed with me for awhile, but it was soon forgotten as I explored the city's beautiful historic district. That day, in spite of the mid-summer heat, there was activity and movement in the narrow streets of Charleston. The sound of horse-drawn carriages could be heard on the cobblestone streets as they toured past elegant homes. At City Market, local artisans sat silently in the sun as they wove their distinctive sweetgrass baskets. Out on the Cooper River, a parade of massive container ships sailed into the Port of Charleston, and each vessel seemed to create its own cooling breeze, bringing salty sea air onshore. Later in the day, as evening arrived on the Battery, I enjoyed a peaceful view of the harbor, with Fort Sumter barely visible in the distance.

The sights and sounds of Charleston seen firsthand that day left me with a distinct impression. Life in the queen city of South Carolina's low country seemed slow and easy—and a thick history book away from any further moments of catastrophe. The story of the quake of 1886 was likely just one of many colorful tales told by a charming and mannerly Southern city. Charleston appeared to be destined to faithfully honor its storied past by serving as a historic time capsule—a duty both pleasant and appropriate for a locale that is arguably the most beautifully preserved community in the United States. Since its founding in 1670, Charleston had survived a succession of hardships and disasters; but in 1986, one hundred years after the earthquake, it seemed primed to cruise carefree into its golden years.

The supporting evidence for this perception was beautifully apparent on every street in the city. Classic architecture had survived three hundred years of weather and war, and antebellum plantations still spread out under the oaks all along the Ashley River. In addition, Charleston had already begun an artistic renaissance that would fortify its claim as the cultural capital of the South. Just three years later however, Charleston would learn that it was not completely free from the demons of its tumultuous past.

On September 21, 1989, Hurricane Hugo stormed ashore with 130 mph winds and a twenty-foot storm surge. The powerful "category-five" storm devastated the South Carolina coast and left seven billion dollars worth of damage in its wake. For the people of Charleston, who had conquered adversity many times, it was probably their most difficult hour. In the aftermath of Hugo, Charleston proved to the world that it

ABOVE: A slender sliver of sand is the partition between water and marsh on the Isle of Palms.

FACING PAGE (TOP): Looking out over the harbor, the monument "To The Confederate Defenders of Charleston" occupies a place of honor on the Battery.

FACING PAGE (BOTTOM): The Citadel has an illustrious and chronicled history that dates back to 1822. Originally chartered "to establish a competent force to act as a municipal guard for the protection of Charleston," the original campus was built around Marion Square. Now formally called The Citadel Military College of South Carolina, the campus moved to its present location in 1922.

was not finished making history just yet. Building by building, the city was rebuilt and restored to its former splendor. This resilient spirit and legendary tenacity remains an integral part of Charleston's identity and it announces with a loud voice that the city will never be an ancient artifact trapped in amber.

In Charleston today, the sophistication of contemporary living mixes seamlessly with the traditions of the Old South. Throughout the city, there are historic sites that date back to the days of muskets and redcoats, as well as modern attractions that represent Charleston's vision of the future. The architectural legacy of Charleston easily captures the imagination, and there are many vintage treasures to enjoy here. A relaxed walk through the National Historic Landmark District reveals a boundless variety of architectural styles and elegance. There are Victorian, Italianate, and Federal-style homes, to name just a few of the varieties, and they are the city's most sought-after sights. Church steeples come into view often, for this is a city known for its houses of devotion and they are the dominant elements of the Charleston skyline. The Battery is a popular place to begin an exploration of the city and see these gorgeous vestiges of a different age. A peek inside a wrought-iron gate in this part of town will likely bring into view a lovely Charleston garden. It is also a common sight to see various stages of home and church restoration as one strolls around the city. Preservation is an ongoing and never-ending process in a city with such an impressive number of aged structures.

Away from downtown, a short drive leads to the scenic river road, home to Charleston's renowned river plantations. Here is where the seeds for the city's success were sown, and where the fortunes that built its opulent mansions were created. Drayton Hall, Magnolia Plantation, and Middleton Place all flourish today, although the planter society that nurtured them is a distant memory. The history of that culture is interpreted and remembered here on the Ashley River, but the most picturesque aspect of these properties is the low-country landscape that remains. Under the twisting limbs of mammoth oak trees, acres of gardens erupt in a profusion of color every spring, wading birds take flight from the shallow wetlands, and slender bridges arch gracefully over the reflective waters of the former rice fields. After a gentle rain in April, this is the most vibrant landscape to be found in the south.

Charleston was settled at the confluence of the Ashley and Cooper Rivers, which is a very strategic location. Over the course of its long history, this setting has provided an immense advantage for the promotion of trade and commerce, but it also attracted the enemy in times of war. Beginning with the days of the founding fathers, Charleston has been a repeated military target. Fort Moultrie on nearby Sullivan's Island was attacked by the British in 1776. The British fleet was driven away that day, but they would return four years later to capture the city and occupy it for two and a half years. In 1860, South Carolina became the first state to leave the Union when an Ordinance of Secession was signed in Charleston. A few months later, the newly created Confederate States of America opened fire on Fort Sumter in Charleston harbor. The city's residents had the distinction of having a front-porch view of the beginning of the Civil War. The fight for control of the city waged on throughout the four-year struggle, but Charleston was fortunate to escape the total devastation that destroyed Columbia, South Carolina's capital city, during the infamous march of General Sherman. Today, visitors can tour these renowned military sights and can also visit Patriots Point, a more contemporary attraction where twentieth-century warfare is centered around the commanding presence of the naval aircraft carrier U.S.S. *Yorktown*.

Charleston complements the elements of its illustrious past with attractions and events that befit a twenty-first-century city with a forward vision. The city is well known as an art enclave, with the annual Spoleto Festival and Southeastern Wildlife Exposition among many of the anticipated events that draw patrons from all over the nation. In recent years, Charleston has refurbished its waterfront, complete with a beautiful aquarium and a fountain-filled park that is popular with residents and visitors alike. The new Cooper River Bridge is the latest project that adds an updated look to the Charleston cityscape.

Amid all the history and culture of Charleston is the lure of the natural landscape. The city is surrounded by fertile marshland, the nursery for shrimp and crab that is nourished twice daily by the incoming tide. Alligators and egrets share a home in the maze of tidal creeks that crisscross the low country. Relief from the heat is found on the coastal islands that protect Charleston, and their names evoke pleasant memories of summers past: Folly Beach, Isle of Palms, and Kiawah and Seabrook Islands are popular places to sunbathe, fish, golf, and fly a kite.

Despite the viciousness that nature can sometimes bestow on coastal communities, Charleston is fortunate to have this fragile and sometimes fierce native environment. Charleston has experienced exciting and turbulent times, much like the landscape that gave it life, but that is only half of the story. The final chapters of this city's narrative, a tale alive today with living history, are still being written on the South Carolina coast. ■

ABOVE: Evening light falls on St. Michael's Episcopal Church, the oldest church edifice in Charleston. In a town that is known for its abundant churches, St. Michael's is perhaps the most celebrated and famous house of worship. The church towers high above the symbolic center of Charleston at the intersection of Meeting and Broad Streets.

RIGHT: In a modern-day vista, storm clouds are scattered by the rising sun as sailboats drift serenely on Charleston Harbor. This view would have been anything but tranquil on September 21, 1989, which is the day Hurricane Hugo struck the city with 130 mph winds and a 20-foot storm surge. The "category five" hurricane left seven billion dollars worth of destruction in its wake and caused severe damage to many historic structures in the city.

ABOVE: Welcoming steps await visitors to Wentworth Mansion, an opulent Charleston inn that is the finest example of Second Empire–style architecture in the city. The mansion was built in 1887 and it was originally home to a wealthy cotton merchant. The inn offers gracious Southern hospitality and a level of refinement that has resulted in its ranking as one of the top fifty luxury hotels in North America.

RIGHT: On a shaded pathway in a Magnolia Plantation garden, a playful sculpture relaxes beneath towering trees and swaying Spanish moss.

FACING PAGE: The Audubon Swamp Garden is a 60-acre sanctuary of blackwater and abundant wildlife on the grounds of Magnolia Plantation. A boardwalk circles the primeval landscape, offering visitors a quiet stroll amid beautiful low-country surroundings.

The Pineapple Fountain glows golden at dawn in Waterfront Park. The pineapple
is known as a symbol of hospitality, thus the flowing fountain is an ideal icon for
a city that is celebrated as a distinguished and genteel travel host.

LEFT: The Edmondston-Alston House is a gracious example of style and elegance on Charleston's East Battery. Built in 1825, the home still contains furniture and artwork that date back over a century and a half to its namesake owners.

BELOW: A twilight view from the Harbor Marina offers a glimpse of pleasure craft and the distant spires of downtown Charleston.

LEFT: Marion Square bustles with activity on Saturday—the traditional day for Charleston's colorful Farmers' Market.

BELOW: A cannon seems poised and ready for action at its position on the Battery. Its barrel points toward Fort Sumter, which received the first shots of the Civil War in 1861.

Randolph Hall is a striking example of the architectural splendor found on the College of Charleston campus. Founded in 1770 and chartered in 1785, it is the thirteenth oldest institution of higher learning in the United States.

LEFT: St. Philip's Church braces for a storm in the historic district. The first service was held here on Easter Sunday 1723 and since that day the structure has survived a procession of natural disasters, including a major fire (1861), an earthquake (1886), and the devastating Hurricane Hugo (1989). It is a fitting symbol of Charleston's resilience and ongoing commitment to historic preservation.

BELOW: Pink is paramount in a photograph of a lovely home on the East Battery.

FACING PAGE: Shrimp boats retire at day's end on Shem Creek, the traditional port for Charleston's shrimping fleet. This Mt. Pleasant waterway is also known as a destination for delicious seafood dining.

RIGHT: Jennifer Capriati at the Family Circle Cup, an annual tennis championship hosted in Charleston. GARY COLEMAN PHOTO

BELOW: Palm trees frame a distant view of the Charleston skyline. The palm is the symbol for the State of South Carolina and is a revered natural emblem found throughout the low country.

FACING PAGE: The Isle of Palms is well known as a refuge from the summer heat of Charleston and is a preferred setting for recreation and waterfront living. At the Isle of Palms marina, visitors are encouraged to "tie up and wind down."

ABOVE: In the historic district, early spring growth begins to conceal the wall of a private home. Hidden behind is one of Charleston's traditional formal gardens.

FACING PAGE: A trio of Charleston homes is framed by overhanging palms and ancient cobblestones.

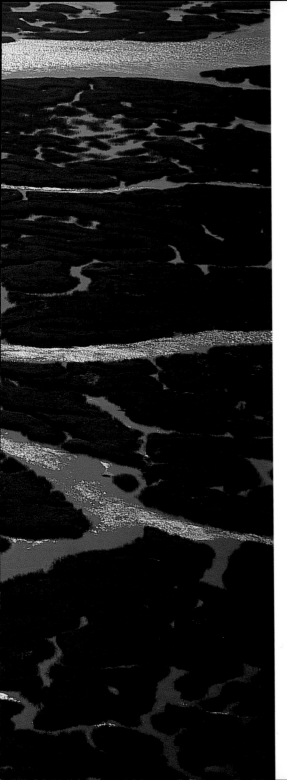

LEFT: Serpentine tidal creeks shimmer in early sunlight as they flow through a maze of coastal Carolina marshland.

BELOW: Beneath the spreading limbs of a live oak, an ornate remembrance for a lost loved one is tendered in Magnolia Cemetery.

An armada of military craft thrills visitors at the Patriots Point Naval and Maritime Museum. The museum is the largest of its kind in the world, with four retired ships anchored on the Cooper River shore. At right is the U.S.S. *Yorktown*, known as the "tip of the spear" for its crucial role in America's victory in the Pacific during World War II.

LEFT: The spire of St. Michael's Episcopal Church rises 186 feet above Charleston, and the towering structure possesses two noteworthy elements. The clock tower is thought to be the oldest functioning timepiece of its kind in the country, and the eight bells hidden within have a unique and fascinating history. They are known as the Bells of St. Michael's.

BELOW: A peek through a Meeting Street gate reveals a charming walled garden that originates at the back doorstep of a lovely Charleston home.

ABOVE: A great egret scans the horizon from a lofty perch. These graceful birds capture their prey in the bountiful waters of local creeks and marshes.

FACING PAGE: A sunrise stroll on Seabrook Island reveals a natural watercolor painting on a canvas of smooth sand.

Inside the First Baptist Church, a window scene symbolizes the traditional religious devotion to simple beliefs.

LEFT: A peacock stands like a sentry on a weathered wall at Middleton Place.

BELOW: The First Baptist Church is the oldest of its denomination in the South. The original founders came from Maine and arrived in Charleston in 1696.

ABOVE: Despite a fearsome reputation, most alligators live peacefully among the residents of the South Carolina coast.

RIGHT: The stillness of a blackwater swamp is palpable on a foggy spring morning.

LEFT: Scott Vandermeer attempts to close out the game for the Charleston RiverDogs.
CHRISTOPHER GINNETT PHOTO

BELOW: Crab cakes are one of the many delicacies of traditional low-country cuisine.

FACING PAGE: Rainbow Row is a Caribbean-colored Charleston landmark found on East Bay Street. The homes, which were built in the early to mid-1700s, once fell into decay but were transformed to their present splendor in the early 1900s.

LEFT: On April 12, 1861, Charleston harbor was ablaze with the fury of cannon fire as the Civil War began. Pictured here from the air, Fort Sumter was the target on that fateful first day. After a bombardment of thirty-three hours, Union Major Robert Anderson surrendered the fort to the Confederates.

BELOW: The timeless elements of Charleston's architectural style are evident on Meeting Street.

FACING PAGE: Washington Square was Charleston's first public park. Found under the light-filtering canopy of live oaks is a peaceful and restful square that is just a few steps away from the hectic activity of Meeting Street.

RIGHT: Stained glass arouses both artistic and religious emotions inside St. Michael's sanctuary.

BELOW: Marion Square glows with a festive spirit when the holiday season is celebrated in Charleston.
PHOTO BY COLEMAN PHOTOGRAPHY

FACING PAGE: Along the Atlantic shoreline, gentle waves interrupt an early sunbeam from a crisp winter sunrise.

ABOVE: The cooling spray of the Waterfront Park fountain is a playful way to retreat from the heat of a Charleston summer.

RIGHT: Fallen crepe myrtle petals are sprinkled among the cobblestones in the historic district.

FACING PAGE: The gardens of Magnolia Plantation are the oldest public gardens in the U.S., and the Long Bridge is one of seven lovely spans that pass over the waters of the former rice fields.

ABOVE: In March and April, Charleston transforms into a tapestry of color as azaleas and other native flowering plants awaken to invigorate the springtime landscape.

RIGHT: An aerial view of the Morris Island Lighthouse illustrates its lonely and precarious position on the coastline. This is the third lighthouse to occupy this location, and it was originally built 1,200 feet from the shoreline.

RIGHT: The Charleston Symphony made its public debut in 1936. It has entertained music lovers since that time with impressive local talent that is enhanced by guest appearances from internationally acclaimed musicians. COURTESY CHARLESTON SYMPHONY

BELOW: A colorful catamaran rests on the shore as a trio of beach walkers wanders by at Folly Beach.

FACING PAGE: A sultry summer evening closes with a dramatic finale as the sun begins to submerge its glowing orb beneath the waters of the Carolina coast.

LEFT: Sweetgrass baskets are a common sight at Charleston's City Market. This art form was brought to the low country from West Africa more than 300 years ago and is practiced by local craftspeople who pass the skill onward from generation to generation.

BELOW: There are not enough superlatives to describe Calhoun Mansion, Charleston's largest private home. This opulent Italianate- and Victorian-style residence has nearly 24,000 square feet of living space and is a popular stop on home tours of the city.

FACING PAGE: White Point Gardens is shrouded in morning mist as a Sunday begins quietly on the Battery.

ABOVE: Along the Ashley River, a great egret wades in shallow water on the fringe of the marsh.

FACING PAGE: The Dock Street Theatre is a well-known Charleston landmark with its wrought-iron balcony and brownstone columns. The structure, which is actually on Church Street, was originally the Planters Hotel back in the early 1800s. The building was restored and converted to a theater and was given its current name in honor of a 1730s theatre that was adjacent to it on the Queen Street (formerly called Dock Street) side of the property.

A pair of kayakers paddles past the slumbering shrimp fleet on picturesque Shem Creek.

ABOVE: Tucked among the trees of the historic district, a side porch is caught up in spring.

RIGHT: Great blue herons stand up to 54 inches tall and can sport a wingspan up to 6 feet. These prehistoric-looking wading birds make their home in waterways all over South Carolina.

ABOVE: An elegant gate is wrought with fine finishing touches in its role as a distinguished entry to a lovely Charleston home.

FACING PAGE: Out in a sweeping expanse of wetland, twilight hues rise up in colorful bands as they welcome a full moon to the eastern sky.

RIGHT: In the shallow water of a reflective pond, a pair of Canada geese share a tranquil setting at Magnolia Plantation.

BELOW: A lasting element found in Charleston homes is the veranda, a place where conversation and a cooling breeze are always welcome.

After a gentle rain, the impression of a Southern spring lingers among dogwoods and azaleas.

From the air, immense vacation homes and sizeable pleasure boats take on a different scale as they congregate along the water's edge on the Isle of Palms.

LEFT: The Gibbes Museum of Art houses an American fine-arts collection with a Charleston perspective.

BELOW: In a union of Far East and low-country essence, Spanish moss drips over a red footbridge in a quiet garden at Magnolia Plantation.

ABOVE: Morning mist and fog muffle the bright-green hues of a salt marsh along the Ashley River.

RIGHT: A dock extends its reach into tinted waters in a landscape seen from high above the Carolina coastline.

A cypress tree
basks in the
warmth of a
mid-winter
sunset.

Classic Charleston
architecture is
exhibited on the
East Battery in
a portrait that
embodies the age-
less dignity of the
city's elegant
homes.

ABOVE: The unique shape of Fort Moultrie comes into view above Sullivan's Island. The fort's history dates back to a British attack by nine warships in 1776.

RIGHT: A chubby cherub adorns a crypt at Magnolia Plantation.

FACING PAGE: A summer morning begins with calm water and muted colors on the Ashley River.

ABOVE: The Nathaniel Russell House was home to a native Rhode Islander who came south to amass a fortune in Charleston. This Federal-style home was constructed in 1808 and is known for the breathtaking elliptical staircase found inside.

FACING PAGE: The idle nets of a shrimp boat await the next day's catch as fog descends on Shem Creek.

The aircraft carrier U.S.S. *Yorktown* is the dominant feature in an aerial view of Charleston Harbor. Patriots Point, the harbor marina, and the Cooper River Bridge share the scene.

Tradition, honor, and history converge on the grounds of the Citadel. On the barrack's checkerboard courtyard, cadets stage military exercises during the school year.

RIGHT: The homes that front East Bay Street display curved doorways and wrought-iron accents with a rainbow of Caribbean color schemes.

BELOW: Beauty is found in the details throughout the historic district.

FACING PAGE: A couple enjoys a sunset view of Charleston Harbor as they relax on the shore at Sullivan's Island.

Kiawah Island is a golfers' paradise with a history for attracting the world's best players. The island has hosted The Ryder Cup and the World Golf Championship, as well as many other prestigious competitions.

RIGHT: Tulips proclaim the arrival of spring—a colorful time in Charleston.

BOTTOM: A primordial low-country scene is centered around a single cypress tree.

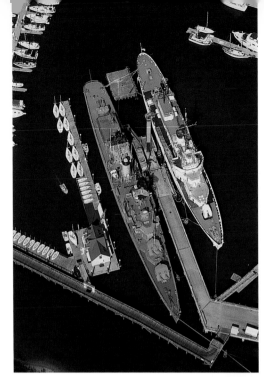

LEFT: These two military ships are gigantic museum pieces at the Patriots Point Naval and Maritime Museum. The destroyer *Laffey* (left) and the Coast Guard Cutter *Ingham* (right) share a berth with smaller, more light-hearted sailing craft.

BELOW: A pair of reenactors welcome visitors to Charleston's Confederate Museum, which is housed in Market Hall. The building, which is adjacent to City Market, was built in 1841 and is also home to the United Daughters of the Confederacy.

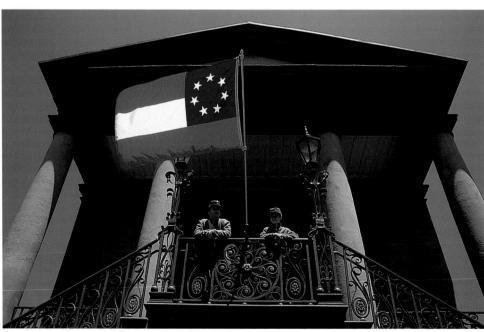

As night falls on Charleston, Broad Street comes alive with motion and activity.

Rain intensifies the colors and softens the features of a springtime scene at Middleton Place.

LEFT: Drayton Hall is a lasting vestige of Charleston's river plantation culture. This beautiful Georgian–Palladian structure was built in 1742, and today it remains the only local manor home of this type to survive the Revolutionary War and the Civil War completely intact.

BELOW: The *Adventure* is a 53-foot trading ketch that is moored at Charles Towne Landing, a state historic site that inteprets the story of the first permanent English settlement in South Carolina.

ABOVE: The Margaret Petterson Gallery is one of several impressive fine-art venues found in Charleston's French Quarter area.

RIGHT: First light at Folly Beach offers the promise of good weather for a summer day spent at the shore.

A sailboat generates a sunlit wake as it glides over the waters of the coastal marsh.

LEFT: The art of precision kite flying is flaunted at Folly Beach.

BELOW: Visitors travel through historic Charleston in style on a carriage ride on the East Battery.

ABOVE: A handsome Charleston home resides vibrantly on a quiet street near the harbor.

RIGHT: The twin spires of the First Scots Presbyterian Church reach up into a brilliant blue sky.

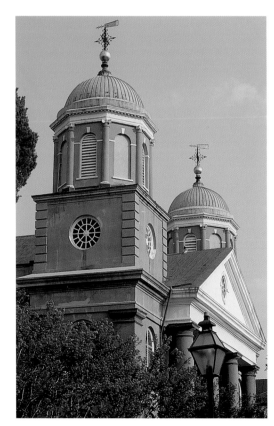

A peek into a Meeting Street garden offers a picture of seasonal transition,
as a hint of spring is evident to an optimistic fountain figurine.

ROBB HELFRICK lives in Atlanta and specializes in location photography for editorial and corporate clients. His photographs have appeared in many national publications, including *Sierra Magazine*, *National Geographic Adventure*, *Audubon*, *Travel Holiday*, *National Geographic Traveler*, *Sky*, and *National Parks*. Close to home, he is a regular contributor to *Atlanta Magazine*. As a sole photographer, Robb is the author of nine photography books, including the Fodor Guide *Georgia*. His work was also featured exclusively in the Farcountry Press books *Savannah Impressions*, *North Carolina Simply Beautiful*, *Atlanta Impressions* and *Charlotte Impressions*. Robb is the recipient of the Len Foote Memorial Award for Conservation Photography, and has won numerous other honors for his work. His photography is sold and exhibited through his Atlanta-based photographic agency, which specializes in images from the American South.